This Page Intentionally Left Blank

The Secrets of Getting Rich

Copyright © 2023

Frank S.D

<u>*Dedication*</u>

To the Almighty, who granted me an alternate chance at life after an accident, to my companions, who partake in the dream of financial freedom beyond traditional family beliefs, to my family, whose unvarying support has been my foundation, and to all my well-provision and fellow campaigners of financial independence, this book is devoted with sincere gratefulness and a hopeful spirit.

<u>About The Author</u>

In the story of life, woven with vestments of events and chances, there is a special boy who stands out. He had a unique trip that changed him a lot. Imagine meeting a youthful boy who came from a simple family, but he did not let that stop him. He faced unanticipated challenges and turned them into openings.

This boy was born into a family where they plodded to make ends meet. He had an elder brother and sister and a family who worked hard to support his daily needs. They tried to balance their dreams with the reality of their limited plutocrat. Indeed though his family had a tough time, the boy loved literacy. But he did not really understand how hard life was for his family. He enjoyed having fun with musketeers and occasionally enjoyed being alone.

One day, commodity really bad happens. The boy had a serious accident and was veritably close to dying. This was really tough for his family, especially because they were formerly having financial problems. But luckily, kind people came to help him recover, indeed though it sounded insolvable.

After surviving the accident, the boy changed a lot. He started learning about finances and how to make them grow. He realized that there were further possibilities beyond what his family knew. He wanted to partake in what he learned with others, so he wrote a book.

In his book, he talks about his trip and what he learned. He wants to help people like him who come from ordinary middle-class families. He believes that we can do further than what people generally suppose, and he wants to show us how to do it.

This boy's story teaches us that indeed when effects are tough, we can still do amazing effects. He wants everyone to know that we have got a lot of implicit inside us. As you read his story, you will see that his trip is an assignment for all of us to believe in ourselves and reach for great effects, indeed if it is not the usual way.

<u>About The Book</u>

Greetings! I am thrilled to introduce myself as the author of a book that holds a special place in my heart. Hailing from a small middle-class family, I embarked on a journey to transform my financial reality and emerge as a beacon of practical wisdom. Today, I am humbled to present to you my book, *"The Secrets of Getting Rich"*.

This book is a testament to my own experiences, struggles, and triumphs as I navigated the intricate world of personal finance. Born out of a sincere desire to share the invaluable lessons I have learned; I have poured my heart and soul into crafting a resource that resonates with individuals from all walks of life. *"The Secrets of Getting Rich"* is a guide that speaks directly to you, my dearest reader! Through relatable stories and relatable challenges, I aim to empower you with the tools you need to elevate your financial standing, just as I did.

The book delves into a range of practical techniques and insights designed to help individuals not only build wealth but also optimize their financial decisions. Drawing from different strategies, real-life examples of successful personalities, and expert knowledge, the book provides actionable steps for readers to take control of their finances and accelerate their path to prosperity. As you turn the pages, you will discover practical strategies to make the most of your resources, manage your finances effectively, and seize opportunities that align with your aspirations. This book is not just a collection of advice; it is a roadmap that weaves together the threads of my personal journey, offering a guiding light for anyone seeking to rewrite their financial narrative.

I welcome you to the world of possibilities and join me on this transformative expedition and enriching voyage with me as we unlock the secrets of financial success together. *"The*

Secrets of Getting Rich" is not just a book; it is a bridge that connects our shared experiences, proving that regardless of our beginnings, we all have the potential to chart a course toward prosperity. Let us take bold steps toward financial freedom, armed with practical experiences and unwavering determination.

<u>Key Themes</u>

Mindset and Habits:

In addition to practical strategies, the book addresses the significance of cultivating a positive financial mindset and espousing habits that support long-term financial success.

Wealth- structure Foundations:

The book lays a strong foundation by introducing abecedarian generalities of particular finance including personal finance, budgeting, effective plutocrat operation, and money management.

Investment Mastery:

Readers are guided through the art of intelligent investing, exploring colorful asset classes, threat operations, and strategies to grow their wealth over time.

Entrepreneurial Mindset:

The author emphasizes the significance of cultivating an entrepreneurial mindset, encouraging compendiums to identify openings, introduce, and produce multiple income streams.

Financial Freedom Blueprint:

The book unveils a roadmap to financial freedom, outlining attainable mileposts and long-term pretensions and goals that align with individual boundaries.

Audience

This book is designed for a diverse audience, catering to individuals at various stages of their financial journey. Whether readers are newcomers seeking to lay a strong financial foundation or experienced investors looking to fine-tune their strategies, *"The Secrets of Getting Rich"* offers valuable guidance and actionable advice.

<u>Warning</u>

Embarking on the journey outlined in this book may lead to changes in your social circle, hobbies, and habits. As you delve into the transformative principles within these pages, you will find yourself prioritizing growth, ambition, and personal development. For instance, one reader who embraced the book's teachings shifted from leisurely TV watching to dedicating time to skill-building, resulting in a network of like-minded individuals and a newfound sense of purpose. While the transformation may challenge your comfort zone, the rewards of enhanced focus, relationships, and achievements are boundless. Prepare for a fulfilling, yet potentially transformative, path ahead.

Content

Introduction

In a world where economic landscapes are constantly shifting and financial aspirations run high, the pursuit of financial prosperity has become a universal aspiration. It is a journey marked by empowerment, strategic planning, and a mindset that embraces growth and abundance. The ability to wield financial resources effectively can impact not only one's personal well-being but also the ability to make meaningful contributions to society. In this comprehensive exploration, we delve into the intricate facets of financial prosperity, unearthing the core principles and strategies that pave the path to enduring affluence including different examples of strategies and real-life success stories across the world.

Unlocking the Door to Financial Prosperity: A Holistic Perspective

The concept of financial prosperity extends far beyond the mere accumulation of wealth; it encompasses a dynamic synergy between mindful choices, strategic planning, and an unwavering commitment to growth. At its essence, financial prosperity emerges as a harmonious blend of an individual's mindset, informed decisions, and the judicious allocation of resources.

An example of a person with a holistic perspective on unlocking the door to financial prosperity could be someone who not only focuses on traditional financial strategies like investing and saving but also places equal importance on their physical and mental well-being. This person might prioritize maintaining a healthy lifestyle, fostering positive relationships, and continuously learning new skills to enhance their overall quality of life, believing that a balanced and healthy foundation contributes to their financial success in the long run.

Mindset: The Foundation of Prosperity

At the heart of every financial endeavor lies the mindset – the lens through which one perceives and interacts with the world of finances. A growth mindset, one that welcomes challenges and learning opportunities, is a pivotal factor in setting the stage for financial prosperity. Individuals who embrace a growth mindset are more inclined to seek out knowledge, adapt to changing circumstances, and turn setbacks into stepping stones.

Consider the case of Sarah, a young entrepreneur who launched a startup amidst economic uncertainty. Instead of succumbing to fear, Sarah's growth mindset propelled her to research, learn from industry veterans, and pivot her business model. Her ability to navigate challenges, coupled with a belief in her own capacity to learn and adapt, eventually led to her company's success and her personal financial well-being.

Strategic Planning: Paving the Path to Prosperity

Strategic planning is the compass that guides one's financial journey. It involves meticulous goal setting, meticulous budgeting, and shrewd decision-making. Wealth accumulation is not haphazard; it requires a well-defined roadmap that accounts for short-term needs and long-term aspirations.

Take John, for instance, a diligent professional who meticulously budgets his income, allocates a portion to investments, and maintains an emergency fund. John's strategic approach ensures he has the resources to weather unforeseen storms while steadily growing his wealth over time. This combination of discipline and foresight has contributed significantly to John's financial prosperity.

Resource Allocation: Nurturing the Seeds of Abundance

Efficient resource allocation involves striking a balance between spending, saving, and investing. It is the art of optimizing one's financial resources to achieve both immediate gratification and long-term growth. By directing resources toward avenues that appreciate over time, individuals can set the stage for lasting prosperity.

Consider Maria, a young professional who meticulously divides her income among necessary expenses, savings, and investments. By adopting a disciplined approach to resource allocation, Maria has not only managed to travel and pursue her passions but has also seen her investments steadily grow, creating a strong foundation for her financial future.

Crafting Your Path to Prosperity

Financial prosperity emerges as a dynamic interplay between mindset, strategic planning, and resource allocation. It is a journey that empowers individuals to transcend limitations, make informed decisions, and seize opportunities that lead to enduring affluence. By fostering a growth mindset, embracing strategic planning, and optimizing resource allocation, individuals can navigate the complex financial landscape with confidence and build a legacy of prosperity that transcends generations. As we embark on this exploration of financial prosperity, let us remember that the true essence of wealth lies not just in the abundance of financial resources, but in the transformative power it holds to shape lives, communities, and futures.

Chapter 1

<u>Developing a Wealth Mindset</u>

In this chapter, we will explore the core principles of developing a wealth mindset. Transforming your thoughts about money is essential for achieving financial success. Let us dive into simple strategies that can help reshape your perspective and pave the way to prosperity.

Believing in Abundance:

Shift from a scarcity mindset to one of abundance. Understand that there are limitless opportunities and resources available. Train your mind to focus on possibilities rather than limitations.

Positive Self-Talk:

Monitor your inner dialogue and replace self-limiting beliefs with empowering statements. Affirmations like *"I attract wealth"* can rewire your thinking and reinforce your wealth-building journey.

Think Positive:

The Power of Positive Thinking is a mindset that focuses on optimism, sanguinity, and formative studies and thoughts. Believing in one's capacities and visioning positive issues can lead to increased provocation, adaptability, and better internal well-being. It is about cultivating a hopeful station and attitude, which can enhance problem-solving skills and attract success. This approach does not guarantee instant results, but it can shape comprehensions, perceptions, behaviors, opportunities and actions, and openings in a more favorable direction.

Surrounding Yourself with Positivity:

Surround yourself with people who share your financial objectives. Connect with those who have a wealth mindset to learn from their experiences and stay motivated.

Goal Setting for Success:

Set clear and achievable financial goals. Break them down into smaller steps to make progress manageable. Goals provide direction and motivation, helping you stay on track. We will discuss more about it in the upcoming chapter.

Embracing Risk and Learning:

Accept that calculated risks are stepping stones to success. Educate yourself about investments, finance, and wealth-building strategies. Knowledge enables you to make sound decisions. Estimate and evaluate your insurance needs, including health, life, disability, and property insurance. Adequate and acceptable coverage protects your financial well-being from unanticipated events.

Gratitude and Generosity:

Practice gratitude daily for your current financial situation. Cultivate a generous spirit by giving back to your community. Gratitude attracts positivity and fosters a sense of abundance.

Overcoming Setbacks:

View challenges as opportunities for growth. Develop resilience so that you can recover from failures stronger than before. Learn from your mistakes and use them to refine your approach.

Visualization and Manifestation:

Visualize your financial success regularly. Imagine your goals as if they are already achieved. Visualization primes your mind for success and reinforces your commitment and it is a potent tool in the arsenal of goal setting. By vividly picturing the attainment of your goals, you reinforce your commitment, evoke positive emotions, and cultivate a deep-seated belief in their feasibility. Visualization serves as a mental rehearsal, preparing you to navigate challenges and seize opportunities with unwavering determination.

Imagine Natalie, an aspiring entrepreneur aiming to launch her own business. Through daily visualization exercises, Natalie envisions her storefront, delighted customers, and a thriving enterprise. This practice not only bolsters her confidence but also subconsciously steers her decisions and actions toward making her vision a reality.

Continuous Self-Improvement:

Commit to lifelong learning. Stay curious and open to new ideas. Invest in your personal and financial development to keep growing.

Acting:

Ultimately, a wealth mindset is meaningless without action. Apply the principles you have learned. Take steps, no matter how small, towards your financial goals every day.

Remember, developing a wealth mindset is a journey. It requires consistent effort and a willingness to challenge your existing beliefs. By adopting these simple strategies, you can gradually shift your mindset and create a foundation for lasting financial abundance.

Consider the story of Thomas Edison, whose grim pursuit of the incandescent light bulb epitomized a growth mindset. Despite facing numerous failures, Edison viewed each reversal as a step closer to success, famously stating, *"I have not failed. I have just set up 10,000 ways that will not work."*

His unwavering belief in his capability to learn and acclimatize eventually led to one of the most transformative inventions in history.

Chapter 2

<u>Goal Setting and Planning for Wealth</u>

In this chapter, we will explore the crucial process of goal setting and planning for wealth. By establishing clear objectives and developing a strategic plan, you will create a roadmap to financial success. Let us dive into simple and effective strategies that will empower you to set meaningful goals and take actionable steps toward achieving them.

The Power of Goal Setting:

Setting goals gives your financial journey direction and purpose. Define both short-term and long-term objectives that are specific, measurable, achievable, relevant, and time-bound (SMART). These clear targets will serve as guideposts for your wealth-building efforts.

The Anatomy of Clear Goals: Specific, Measurable, Achievable, Relevant, Time-Bound (SMART):

To be effective, goals must adhere to the SMART framework, ensuring they are Specific, Measurable, Achievable, Relevant, and Time-Bound. This approach transforms aspirations into tangible targets, rendering them actionable and providing a robust framework for assessment and adjustment. S.M.A.R.T. goals are a powerful framework for crafting clear, and meaningful objectives. When applied to financial goals, this methodology provides a structured approach that enhances focus, accountability, and the likelihood of successful wealth creation. Let us delve into how to set S.M.A.R.T. financial goals:

Specific(S)- ***Define Precise Objectives***: Define goals with clarity and precision. Rather than aiming to "save money," specify a concrete amount to save within a defined timeframe, such as "$10,000 which is almost

8,28,068.00 Rs. in a high-yield savings account within two years. Begin by articulating your financial goals with specificity. Clearly state what you want to achieve, why it matters to you, and how you intend to accomplish it. Avoid vague statements and focus on concrete outcomes. For example, instead of saying "I want to save money," specify "I aim to save $10,000 over the next two years for a down payment on a house."

Measurable(M)- *Quantify Your Goals*: Establish metrics to gauge progress and success. This could involve tracking the percentage of your goal achieved or monitoring the growth of an investment portfolio. Quantifying your financial goals provides a clear yardstick for tracking progress and measuring success. Assign numerical values to your objectives so that you can gauge your accomplishments over time. Continuing from the previous example, make it measurable by stating "I will save $10,000 or Rs. 8,32,254.00 by contributing $417 or almost Rs. 34,704.00 per month to a dedicated savings account."

Achievable(A)- *Set Realistic Targets*: Goals should be ambitious yet realistic. While aiming to double your income in a year might be challenging, pursuing a 20% increase could be more feasible and motivating. Ensure that your financial goals are attainable within your current circumstances. Consider your income, expenses, time commitments, and resources when setting your objectives. If your monthly budget allows for a $417 almost Rs. 34,704.00 contribution, the goal is achievable. However, setting an unrealistic amount that strains your finances could lead to frustration and demotivation.

Relevant(R)- *Align with Your Aspirations***:** Align goals with your broader financial aspirations and life values. Ensure that pursuing the goal contributes meaningfully to your overall financial well-being. Your financial goals should align with your values, and life priorities, and ask yourself if the goal is relevant to your long-term vision. In the context of saving for a down payment on a house, consider if homeownership is a significant life goal for you and if it fits into your overall financial plan.

Time-Bound(T)- *Set a Clear Timeline***:** Establish and set a specific and definitive timeframe within which you intend to achieve your financial goal. A well-defined timeline creates a sense of urgency and accountability, motivating you to stay on track moreover prevents procrastination, spurring consistent action. Incorporating the time-bound element, your goal becomes "I will save $10,000 or Rs. 8,32,254.00 by contributing $417 almost Rs. 34,704.00 per month to a dedicated savings account over the next 24 months, with the aim of having a down payment ready within two years."

Monitoring and Celebrating Progress:

After setting your S.M.A.R.T. financial goals, regularly monitor your progress. Review your goals periodically, track your savings, and assess whether you are on target to achieve your objectives within the defined timeline. Celebrate milestones along the way to maintain motivation and reinforce your commitment. Each step closer to your financial goal is a testament to your dedication and discipline.

Regular Review, Adaptability, and Adjustments:

Life is dynamic, and circumstances may change and different life events, economic shifts, or personal priorities may necessitate revisions to your plan. Be prepared to adapt your

S.M.A.R.T. financial goals if necessary. If your income increases, you may consider increasing your monthly contributions to achieve your goal faster. Alternatively, unexpected expenses may require adjusting your timeline. Consistently assess your progress and make necessary adjustments to your plan. Life circumstances and financial markets can change, so adapt your strategy accordingly. Regularly review your personalized wealth plan to assess progress, adjust goals, and adapt to changing circumstances.

Identifying Your "Why":

Understand your motivations for pursuing wealth. Is it to provide for your family, achieve financial freedom, or create a legacy? Defining your "why" will fuel your determination and help you stay committed when challenges arise.

Creating Financial Milestones:

Divide your major ambitions into smaller, more manageable benchmarks. These smaller victories will give you a sense of progress and keep you motivated along the way.

Prioritizing Goals:

Not all goals are created equal. Prioritize your objectives based on their importance and alignment with your overall financial vision. Focus on a few key goals to prevent overwhelm and maintain focus.

A.   Short-Term Goals: Navigating the Present

Short-term goals serve as the navigational compass of your daily life. They are the incremental steps that propel you forward, foster motivation, and provide a sense of accomplishment. While these goals often have immediate or near-future outcomes, their significance extends far beyond the present moment.

1. **Focus and Motivation**: Short-term goals channel your attention and energy toward specific tasks, helping you stay focused and motivated. They break down larger ambitions into manageable chunks, making progress tangible and fostering a sense of achievement

2. **Building Momentum**: Achieving short-term goals creates a sense of momentum. Each accomplishment fuels your confidence, setting the stage for further progress and propelling you toward more ambitious endeavors.

3. **Adaptability:** Short-term goals allow flexibility to respond to changing circumstances and seize emerging opportunities. They help you stay agile and adjust your course as needed.

4. **Skill Development:** Pursuing short-term goals often involves acquiring new skills, expanding your knowledge, and enhancing your capabilities. This continuous learning contributes to personal and professional growth.

B.   Long-Term Goals: Envisioning Your Future

Long-term goals are the visionary anchors that provide direction and purpose to your journey. They represent the larger narrative you are crafting for your life and encapsulate your deepest aspirations.

1. **Strategic Alignment:** Long-term goals provide strategic alignment for your short-term efforts. They ensure that your daily actions are coherent and meaningful, guiding you toward a unified vision of success.

2. **Sustained Motivation:** The pursuit of long-term goals requires persistence and endurance. They fuel your motivation by reminding you of the overarching purpose behind your actions, even during challenging times.

3. **Legacy and Fulfillment:** Long-term goals contribute to your sense of fulfillment by allowing you to work toward meaningful accomplishments over an extended period. They offer the satisfaction of leaving a lasting legacy.
4. **Holistic Well-Being:** Long-term goals encourage you to consider various dimensions of well-being, including financial, emotional, and relational aspects. They prompt you to make holistic decisions that align with your overarching objectives.
5. **Resilience:** Long-term goals cultivate resilience by encouraging you to persevere through setbacks and fluctuations. They instill the belief that setbacks are temporary roadblocks on the path to ultimate success.

C. Harmonizing the Two:

The symbiotic relationship between short-term and long-term goals is essential for balanced growth and sustained success. Short-term goals provide immediate purpose and gratification, while long-term goals infuse your journey with a sense of direction and legacy. When aligned effectively, these two types of goals propel you toward a future where the pursuit of meaningful achievements is both purposeful and rewarding. As you navigate the intricate dance between short-term steps and long-term visions, you craft a narrative of personal and professional evolution that resonates with purpose and enduring fulfillment.

Developing Your Wealth Plan:

Craft a comprehensive plan outlining the steps you need to take to achieve your goals. Include strategies for income generation, saving, investing, and managing debt. Your plan should be flexible to accommodate changes and adjustments.

Budgeting for Success:

Make a budget that accounts for your income, expenses, and savings goals. A well-structured budget will help you allocate funds effectively, avoid overspending, and channel resources toward wealth-building activities.

Debt Management:

Develop a strategy for managing and reducing debt. Prioritize paying off high-interest debts while maintaining a manageable level of good debt that can contribute to your financial growth. We will discuss it in depth about it in upcoming chapters.

Diversifying Investments & Asset Allocation:

Explore various investment options, such as stocks, real estate, or retirement accounts, to grow your wealth. Diversification spreads risk and increases the potential for long-term gains. Craft an estate plan that includes a will, power of attorney, and, if necessary, trusts. Ensure your assets are distributed according to your wishes and minimize potential estate taxes.

- Diversifying across different investment vehicles, like mutual funds, bonds, and real estate, helps spread risk and reduce the impact of poor performance in any single asset class.
- Asset allocation involves determining the optimal mix of investments based on your risk tolerance, investment horizon, and financial goals.

Seeking Professional Guidance:

Consider consulting with financial advisors or experts to gain insights tailored to your situation. Their expertise can help you make informed decisions and optimize your wealth-building approach. Consider consulting tax professionals and estate planners to ensure your personalized wealth plan is well-informed and tailored to your unique circumstances.

By setting well-defined goals and crafting a strategic wealth plan, you are laying a strong foundation for financial success. Remember, consistency and discipline are key. As you take intentional steps toward your goals, you will gain confidence and experience the tangible results of your efforts. Keep your vision in mind, stay committed, and enjoy the journey to financial prosperity.

Chapter 3

<u>Mastering Budgeting and Efficient Spending</u>

In this chapter, we will explore the essential concepts of budgeting and efficient spending to help you manage your finances effectively and work towards your wealth-building goals. By understanding where your money goes and making intentional spending choices, you can create a solid financial foundation. Let us dive into simple and practical strategies for mastering budgeting and optimizing your spending habits.

The Importance of Budgeting:

A budget is your financial roadmap, guiding your spending decisions and ensuring your money aligns with your goals. Recognize that budgeting empowers you to take control of your finances and make informed choices. It serves as the cornerstone of sound financial management, enabling individuals to take control of achieving their goals and build a solid foundation for long-term wealth accumulation. By mastering the art of budgeting and adopting strategies for efficient spending, you pave the way for financial empowerment and a brighter financial future. Dedicate a portion of your income to savings, investments, and regularly track your expenses to ensure alignment with your budget accordingly.

Assessing Your Income:

Start by calculating your total income, including your salary, freelance work, and other sources. Having a clear picture of your earnings is the foundation of effective budgeting.

Tracking Your Expenses:

Record all your expenses for a month to understand your spending patterns. Categorize expenses into essentials (housing, utilities, groceries, rent) and discretionary (entertainment, dining out). This snapshot will help identify areas for potential savings.

Creating Categories:

Segment your expenses into specific categories, such as housing, transportation, groceries, entertainment, and savings. This organization will give you a detailed view of your financial habits.

Prioritize Needs vs. Wants:

Distinguish between essential needs and discretionary wants. Allocate your resources toward meeting needs while minimizing spending on wants. This practice enhances financial discipline and ensures that your essentials are covered.

Embrace the 50/30/20 Rule:

Consider the 50/30/20 rule: Allocate 50% of your income to essentials & necessities (housing, utilities, groceries), 30% to discretionary spending (entertainment, dining out), and 20% to savings and debt repayment. This balanced approach ensures financial stability while allowing for some flexibility in spending. Adjust these percentages based on your goals and lifestyle.

Setting Spending Limits:

Based on your income and financial goals, allocate a set amount to each area. Prioritize essentials and allocate a portion for discretionary spending.

Limit Impulse Spending:

Practice mindful spending by avoiding impulse purchases. Before buying, assess whether the item aligns with your needs or long-term goals. Consider implementing a waiting period (24 hours) before making non-essential purchases and practice a *"24-hour rule"*. Wait a day before buying to determine if the item is truly necessary.

Cutting Unnecessary Expenses:

Determine where you can save money without affecting your quality of life. Minimize impulse purchases and prioritize needs over wants.

Create an Emergency Fund:

Build an emergency fund equivalent to three to six months' worth of living expenses. This safety net cushions you against unexpected financial shocks, reducing the need for high-interest debt in emergencies. We will discuss it in depth in the next chapter.

Use Envelope or Cash System:

Allocate cash into envelopes dedicated to specific and discretionary spending categories (groceries, entertainment). Place a predetermined amount of cash in each envelope for the month. Once the envelope is empty, and the money is gone, you are done with that category accordingly refrain from spending in that category until the next budget cycle.

Automate Savings and Investments:

Set up automatic transfers to your savings and investment accounts. This habit ensures that a portion of your income is consistently allocated toward your financial goals before discretionary spending. This "pay yourself first" approach ensures consistent contributions towards your financial goals.

Comparison Shop:

When making significant purchases, compare prices and research deals to ensure you are getting the best value. Online tools and price comparison websites can help you make informed decisions. Before making purchases, compare prices from different sources. Look for deals, discounts, and consider buying generic brands to save money without compromising quality.

Define Your Values and Priorities:

Identify your core values and financial priorities. Clarifying what truly matters to you allows you to align your spending with your aspirations and avoid frivolous expenses.

Prioritize Quality Over Quantity:

Choose quality over quantity when making purchases. Investing in well-made, durable items might have a higher upfront cost but can save you money in the long run.

Shop with a List:

Create shopping lists for groceries, household items, and other essentials. Stick to the list to avoid spontaneous purchases that can derail your budget.

Embrace Minimalism:

Adopt a minimalist mindset by focusing on what truly adds value to your life. Eliminate clutter and unnecessary possessions, and prioritize experiences over material possessions.

Practice the 30-Day Rule:

For non-essential purchases, wait 30 days before buying. If you still want the item after the waiting period, consider its value and impact on your budget.

Utilize Cash-Back Rewards and Discounts:

Take advantage of cash-back rewards, loyalty programs, and discounts when making purchases. These perks can provide additional savings over time.

DIY and Repurpose:

Engage in do-it-yourself (DIY) projects, repairs, or repurposing items instead of buying new ones. This approach can save money and enhance your creativity.

Meal Planning and Cooking at Home:

Prepare meals at home and plan your menus. This saves money while simultaneously encouraging healthier eating habits.

Consider Second-Hand Purchases:

When possible, opt for second-hand items or thrift stores for clothing, furniture, and other goods. You can find quality items at a fraction of the cost.

Practice Mindful Spending:

Before each purchase, ask yourself if the item aligns with your budget, values, and financial goals. Mindful spending helps you make intentional choices that support your overall well-being. Please make intentional choices about how you use your financial resources. By adopting mindful spending habits and applying strategic techniques, you can optimize your budget, achieve your goals, and create a more fulfilling and financially secure future.

Avoid Emotional Spending:

Be mindful of emotional triggers that lead to impulse spending. Recognize when stress, boredom, or other emotions influence your purchasing decisions.

Revisiting and Adjusting:

Regularly review your budget to assess your progress. Adjust your spending limits and categories as needed to stay aligned with your financial goals.

Rewarding Yourself:

Celebrate your achievements & successes along the way! Set budget milestones and reward yourself when you meet them. This positive reinforcement keeps you motivated to stick to your budget. Each milestone reached and financial goal achieved is a testament to your commitment and discipline.

Celebrate Smart Choices:

Acknowledge and celebrate your smart spending choices. Each decision to prioritize meaningful expenses over impulsive ones is a step toward financial empowerment.

Review Subscriptions and Memberships:

Regularly assess subscriptions, memberships, and recurring expenses. Cancel or renegotiate those that no longer provide value or align with your priorities.

Continuously Educate Yourself:

Stay informed about personal finance best practices, budgeting techniques, and efficient spending strategies. Continuous education empowers you to make informed decisions and adapt to changing financial circumstances.

Examine Your Spending Patterns:

Review your spending habits over the past few months. Analyze where your money is going and identify areas where you can reduce discretionary spending.

Evaluate Your Savings and Investments:

Assess your savings accounts, investment portfolios, and retirement funds. Determine whether your current savings align with your goals and if your investments are performing as expected.

Understand Your Insurance Coverage:

Review your insurance policies, including health, life, auto, and property insurance. Ensure you have adequate coverage to protect against unexpected events.

Consider Tax Implications:

Understand how taxes impact your financial situation. Be aware of your tax bracket, deductions, credits, and any upcoming tax liabilities.

Reflect on Your Financial Mindset:

Examine your beliefs and attitudes about money. Your financial mindset influences your behavior and decisions. Identify any limiting beliefs that may be affecting your financial choices.

Create a Financial Snapshot:

Compile all this information into a comprehensive financial snapshot. This document serves as a reference point for making financial decisions and tracking progress toward your goals.

Seek Professional Advice:

If you encounter challenges & if needed, consult with financial advisors, accountants, or other professionals to gain a deeper understanding of complex financial matters, situations or to develop a tailored financial plan & guidance

Empowerment through Knowledge:

Understanding your financial situation is a transformative act of empowerment. It enables you to take charge of your financial destiny, make informed decisions, and proactively shape a future marked by financial security and abundance. As you delve into the depths of your financial landscape, remember that knowledge is the compass that guides your journey toward lasting prosperity. Smart and conscious spending is a journey of self-awareness, intentionality, and empowerment. By implementing these strategies, you elevate your financial well-being, strengthen your ability to achieve your goals and cultivate a sense of abundance that extends beyond material possessions. Remember that each thoughtful spending decision is a declaration of your commitment to a future marked by financial security, fulfillment, and lasting prosperity.

By mastering budgeting and adopting efficient spending habits, you are taking significant strides toward achieving your wealth-building objectives. Remember, budgeting is a tool that empowers you to make intentional financial decisions and prioritize what truly matters to you. As you continue to refine your budget and spending practices, you will create a solid financial foundation that supports your journey to lasting prosperity.

Chapter 4

<u>The Art of Saving and Investing</u>

In this chapter, we will explore the art of saving and investing, two essential factors of building wealth over time. By cultivating a habit of chastened saving and making informed investment choices, you can maximize the excrescency of your financial growth Allows claw into simple yet operative strategies for saving and inoculating wisely.

The Foundation of Saving:

Saving is the foundation of financial stability and excrescency. It provides a security net for emergencies and a source of finances for future investments. Recognize the significance of saving as a pivotal step toward scoring and achieving your financial pretensions.

Setting Saving pretensions:

Outline your saving objects, similar to creating an emergency fund, saving for a down payment on a house, or financing your retirement. Having special goals gives your savings efforts instruction and purpose.

Pay Yourself First:

Set away a portion of your earnings for savings as soon as you received them. Automate transfers to a separate savings account regard to insure harmonious benefactions.

Creating an Emergency Fund:

Prioritize building an emergency fund that covers three to six months' worth of your living expenses including specific needs. This fund deposit provides a security or safety net during unanticipated situations, helping you avoid financial lapses. An emergency fund is a financial cushion that provides you with peace of mind and resilience in the face of unexpected expenses or life's uncertainties. By diligently saving for emergencies, you create a safety net that safeguards your financial well-being and empowers you to navigate challenges with confidence. Here is a comprehensive guide to building and maintaining an emergency fund:

1. Understand the Importance:

An emergency fund is essential to cover unexpected expenses, such as medical bills, car repairs, job loss, or home repairs, without derailing your financial stability.

2. Set a Savings Goal:

Aim to build an emergency fund equivalent to three to six months' worth of living expenses. This ensures you have adequate coverage during unexpected situations.

3. Start Small and Be Consistent:

Begin by setting aside a small portion of your income each month. Consistency is key, even if your initial contributions are modest.

4. Create a Separate Account:

Open a separate savings account specifically designated for your emergency fund. This separation helps prevent the fund from being accidentally spent on non-emergencies.

5. Automate Savings:

Set up automatic transfers from your main account to your emergency fund account. Automating savings ensures that you consistently contribute without needing to remember.

6. Prioritize Fund Growth:

As your financial situation improves, strive to increase your emergency fund beyond the initial goal to provide an even stronger safety net.

7. Budget for Your Fund:

Treat your emergency fund as a regular expense in your budget. Allocate a portion of your income toward building and maintaining this fund.

8. Use Windfalls Wisely:

Direct unexpected windfalls, such as tax refunds or bonuses, into your emergency fund to accelerate its growth.

9. Avoid Temptation:

Commit to using the emergency fund only for genuine emergencies. Temptations to dip into the fund for non-urgent purposes should be avoided.

10. Review and Adjust:

Periodically reassess your emergency fund goal based on changes in your financial situation, family size, and lifestyle.

11. Build Fund Before Paying Off Low-Interest Debt:

While paying off high-interest debt is a priority, consider building a basic emergency fund before aggressively tackling low-interest debt.

12. Maintain Liquid Assets:

Keep the emergency fund in a liquid account, such as a savings or money market account, to ensure quick access when needed.

13. Refill the Fund:

After using the emergency fund, make it a priority to replenish it as soon as possible to maintain your financial security.

14. Avoid Investment Risks:

An emergency fund is not meant for investment. Keep it in a low-risk, easily accessible account to ensure you can access the funds when required.

15. Celebrate Financial Milestones:

Acknowledge and celebrate each milestone as you build your emergency fund. Every contribution brings you closer to greater financial security.

16. Empowerment through Preparedness:

Building an emergency fund is a fundamental step toward achieving financial security and peace of mind. This fund provides you with the ability to navigate unexpected challenges without derailing your financial progress. By consistently and deliberately saving for emergencies, you fortify your financial foundation and pave the way for a future marked by resilience, stability, and the empowerment to overcome life's unexpected twists and turns.

Using Retirement Accounts:

Use retirement accounts similar to 401(k)s and IRAs. These accounts give tax advantages while also allowing your investments to boost over time. Contribute constantly to secure your financial future.

Compound Interest:

Understand the power of compound interest, where your money earns interest on both the original amount and the accreted interest.

Manners or Types of Investments:

Probe different investment options, including stocks, bonds, mutual funds, and real estate. Diversifying your total investments in different sectors and areas usually spreads risk and increases the potential for returns.

Risk Tolerance:

Assess your risk tolerance before investing. Consider your position and comfort level with potential fluctuations in the value of your leaguers. Your risk and investment opinions will be told by your threat forbearance and risk tolerance.

Start small scale and gradationally boost:

Begin with a manageable quantum of money and gradationally boost your investment benefactions as your financial situation improves. Consistency and thickness are crucial to long-tenure success.

Dollar or Rupee Cost Averaging:

Learn about cost averaging and start practicing by investing a set amount of money at regular intervals, then only can exercise cost averaging. This program helps reduce the jolt of repeated market fluctuations and oscillations on your investments.

Research and Education:

Educate yourself about different nonidentical investment options and strategies. Make informed decisions based on your financial goals and risk tolerance. Financial education bridges the chasm of financial illiteracy, transforming ignorance into empowerment. It empowers individuals to decipher complex financial jargon, comprehend intricate concepts, and make informed choices that align with their aspirations and values. This knowledge arms them against the perils of predatory lending, debt traps, and exploitative financial products, fostering a shield of resilience against financial vulnerability. Let us take a few examples:

- ➢ Consider Eloni, a recent college graduate entering the workforce. Armed with comprehensive financial education, Eloni adeptly evaluates her employee benefits, navigates retirement account options, and crafts a budget that prioritizes savings and debt reduction. Her knowledge-based decisions empower her to start her financial journey on a strong footing, sidestepping pitfalls that could impede her progress.
- ➢ Take Joseph, for instance, who once regarded investing as an enigma. Through financial education, he not only comprehends the principles of diversification and risk management but also feels confident in his ability to construct an investment portfolio that facilitates long-term wealth accumulation. His transformation from a hesitant novice to a savvy investor underscores the transformative power of financial education.
- ➢ Imagine Beatriz, a single mother juggling multiple financial responsibilities. Armed with financial literacy, Beatriz effectively manages her budget, identifies ways to reduce unnecessary expenses, and builds an emergency fund. Her adept financial management not only bolsters her confidence but also enhances her ability to provide for her family's well-being and plan for their future.

Seeking Professional guidance:

Consider consulting with a financial advisor to receive personalized guidance tailored and acclimatized to your situation. An expert can help and support you to create an investment portfolio aligned with your objectives.

Long-Term Perspective:

Approach investing with a long-term perspective. The value of investments can fluctuate in the short term, but historically, the market tends to grow over time.

Regular Review and Adjustments:

Monitor your investment portfolio periodically and adjust as needed and demanded. Rebalance your portfolio to maintain your desired asset allocation.

Patience and Discipline:

Exercise patience and discipline as you navigate the world of investing. Avoid making hasty decisions based on short-term market fluctuations.

By mastering the art of saving and investing, you are setting yourself up for long-term financial success. Saving provides a safety net and a foundation for investing, while wise investment choices can help your wealth grow exponentially over time. Remember, the journey to financial prosperity requires commitment, education, and a willingness to adapt your strategies as needed. As you build your investment portfolio and watch your savings grow, you will be one step closer to achieving your wealth-building goals.

Balancing Patience and Persistence:

While tracking progress and adjusting is crucial, remember that achieving significant goals often requires both patience and persistence. Be prepared for periods of gradual progress, setbacks, and challenges. Your ability to remain steadfast in the face of adversity, coupled with your willingness to adapt and refine your strategies, positions you for long-term success.

Chapter 5

<u>Entrepreneurship and Multiple Income Streams</u>

In this chapter, we will dive into the exciting world of entrepreneurship and the concept of creating multiple income streams. By harnessing your skills and creativity, you can build a diversified portfolio of income sources that contribute to your financial well-being. Let us explore simple yet effective strategies for embracing entrepreneurship and developing multiple streams of income.

The Entrepreneurial Mindset:

Entrepreneurship is about identifying opportunities, taking calculated risks, and creating value. Cultivate a mindset of innovation, resilience, and a willingness to learn from both successes and failures.

Discovering Your Passion and Skills:

Start by identifying your strengths, passions, and skills. Consider how these attributes can be leveraged to provide value to others and create income-generating opportunities.

Identifying Business Ideas:

Brainstorm business ideas that align with your passions and skills. Look for gaps in the market, unmet needs, or ways to improve existing products or services.

Validating Your Ideas:

Before fully committing, validate your business ideas by conducting market research and seeking feedback from potential customers. This process ensures that there's demand for your product or service.

Creating a Business Plan:

Develop a comprehensive business plan outlining your business goals, target audience, marketing strategies, and financial projections. A well-structured plan provides a roadmap for your entrepreneurial journey.

Starting Small:

Begin with a lean approach, focusing on the essentials to launch your business. As your venture grows, you can invest more resources and expand your offerings.

Leveraging Online Platforms:

Make use of online tools to reach a larger audience. Create a website, utilize social media, and explore e-commerce to connect with potential customers.

Freelancing and Consulting:

Offer your skills as a freelancer or consultant in areas such as writing, design, marketing, or coaching. Freelancing allows you to generate income while leveraging your expertise.

Passive Income Streams:

Explore passive income opportunities, such as royalties from books, digital products, rental income, or dividends from investments. Passive income can provide financial stability over time. Creating passive income streams and achieving a balance between risk and rewards are crucial aspects of entrepreneurial success. Passive income allows you to generate earnings with less active involvement, providing financial stability and freedom. However, managing risk is essential to protect your investments and ensure sustainable growth. Here is how to create passive income streams and strike a balance between risk and rewards as an entrepreneur:

1. Real Estate Investments:

Rental properties, real estate crowdfunding, or real estate investment trusts (REITs) can generate rental income and potential property appreciation.

2. Dividend Stocks:

Invest in dividend-paying stocks to earn regular income from dividend distributions.

3. Peer-to-Peer Lending:

Participate in peer-to-peer lending platforms to earn interest income by lending to individuals or businesses.

4. Digital Products:

Create and sell digital products such as e-books, online courses, software, or stock photography.

5. Affiliate Marketing:

Promote products or services through affiliate marketing and earn commissions on sales generated through your referrals.

6. Create a YouTube Channel or Blog:

Build an audience and monetize your content through ad revenue, sponsorships, and affiliate marketing.

7. Automated Online Businesses:

Set up e-commerce stores, drop shipping, or print-on-demand businesses that can operate with minimal hands-on management.

8. Royalties and Licensing:

License your creative works, such as music, art, or designs, to earn royalties from their use.

Side Hustles:

Consider starting a side hustle alongside your main job. Side hustles allow you to experiment with different income streams and build your entrepreneurial skills gradually.

Investing in Education:

Invest in your personal and professional development to enhance your entrepreneurial skills. Courses, workshops, and online resources can help you stay informed and adapt to market trends.

Networking and Partnerships:

Build a strong network by connecting with other entrepreneurs, mentors, and potential collaborators. Partnerships can provide new opportunities and expand your reach.

Scaling Your Ventures:

As your income streams grow, explore ways to scale your ventures. This may involve hiring employees, outsourcing tasks, or expanding your product/service offerings.

Managing Your Time Effectively:

Balancing multiple income streams requires efficient time management. Prioritize tasks, set boundaries, and allocate time to each venture based on its potential return.

Embracing Flexibility:

Entrepreneurship and multiple income streams offer flexibility and the potential to pursue your passions. Embrace the freedom to design your work schedule and lifestyle.

By embracing entrepreneurship and developing multiple income streams, you are creating a resilient and dynamic financial foundation. Whether through starting a business, freelancing, or pursuing passive income opportunities, diversifying your income sources can enhance your financial security and open doors to new possibilities. Remember, each income stream may start small, but with dedication, creativity, and a willingness to adapt, you can build a thriving portfolio of ventures that contribute to your long-term wealth and success.

Chapter 6

<u>Debt Management and Financial Literacy</u>

In this chapter, we will explore the critical topics of debt management and financial literacy, both of which are essential for achieving lasting financial well-being. By understanding how to effectively manage debt and acquiring the knowledge to make informed financial decisions, you can navigate your financial journey with confidence. Let us delve into simple and actionable strategies for mastering debt management and building strong financial literacy. By mastering debt management and building strong financial literacy, you are equipping yourself with the tools to make informed decisions. Whether it is managing debt responsibly, understanding investment opportunities, or planning for the future, your knowledge and skills will empower you to navigate your financial journey with confidence. Remember, financial literacy is a lifelong endeavor, and the more you learn and apply, the better equipped you will be to achieve your endeavor's wealth-building goals.

Understanding how to effectively manage debt and improving your financial literacy empowers you to take control of your finances, reduce financial stress, and work toward your long-term goals.

Understanding Different Types of Debt:

Begin by recognizing the various types of debt, including good (investment in assets like education or real estate) and bad (high-interest consumer debt). Differentiate between the two to make informed borrowing decisions.

Creating a Debt Repayment Plan:

Create a repayment plan if you already have debt. Prioritize high-interest debt while making minimum payments on other obligations. As you pay off debts, allocate those funds toward the next debt on your list.

Budgeting for Debt Repayment:

Incorporate debt repayment into your budget. Allocate a portion of your income to systematically reduce your debt over time. Consistency is key to achieving your debt reduction goals.

Negotiating with Creditors:

If you are struggling with debt payments, consider negotiating with creditors for better terms, such as reduced interest rates or extended repayment schedules.

Debt Consolidation:

Consider consolidating multiple debts into a single loan with a lower interest rate to simplify payments and reduce overall interest costs.

Avoiding New Debt:

While repaying existing debt, avoid accumulating new debt. Embrace a cash-based approach for discretionary spending to prevent adding to your debt load.

Avoiding Debt Traps:

Proper debt management helps you avoid excessive debt accumulation and high-interest payments that can hinder your financial progress.

Financial Freedom:

By managing debt, you free up resources that can be directed toward savings, investments, and achieving financial goals.

Exploring Financial Literacy:

Financial literacy is the foundation for making informed financial decisions. Educate yourself about budgeting, saving, investing, taxes, and other relevant financial topics.

Reading Personal Finance Resources:

Invest time in reading books, articles, and online resources that cover personal finance. Gaining insights from experts can empower you to make informed choices.

Taking Online Courses:

Explore online courses or workshops that offer in-depth knowledge about specific financial topics, such as investing, retirement planning, or debt management.

Consulting Financial Advisors:

Consider seeking guidance from financial advisors who can provide personalized recommendations based on your financial situation and goals.

Understanding Credit Scores:

Learn about credit scores and their impact on your financial life. Maintain good credit habits to secure favorable terms on loans and financial opportunities. Responsible debt management contributes to a positive credit history and a higher credit score, which can impact your ability to secure loans and favorable interest rates.

Exploring Investment Options:

Expand your understanding of investment options, such as stocks, bonds, mutual funds, and retirement accounts. Make informed choices that align with your risk tolerance and goals

Building a Diversified Portfolio:

As your financial literacy grows, focus on building a diversified investment portfolio that balances risk and potential returns.

Continuously Updating Your Knowledge:

Financial literacy is an ongoing journey. Stay curious and committed to learning as financial markets and regulations evolve. The importance of Financial Literacy is:

1. **Informed Decision-Making**: Financial literacy enables you to make well-informed decisions about savings, investments, borrowing, and budgeting.
2. **Avoiding Scams:** Financial literacy helps you recognize and avoid scams, fraud, and predatory lending practices.
3. **Goal Achievement:** A solid understanding of personal finance allows you to set and achieve financial goals effectively.

We can adopt different strategies for enhancing our financial knowledge which have been listed below:

a. Educational Resources:

-Books: Read personal finance books written by experts to gain insights into various financial topics.

-Online Articles: Explore reputable financial websites and blogs that provide informative articles on budgeting, investing, and debt management.

-Online Courses: Enroll in online courses or webinars that cover specific financial topics.

b. Financial Workshops and Seminars:

-Attend local workshops or seminars offered by financial institutions, community organizations, or universities.

c. Financial Advisors:

-Consult with certified financial advisors to receive personalized guidance tailored to your specific financial situation and goals.

d. Mobile Apps and Tools:

-Use financial apps and tools that help you track expenses, create budgets, and manage your finances effectively.

e. Community Resources:

-Check if your local community offers financial literacy workshops, classes, or resources.

f. Government and Non-profit Organizations:

-Explore resources provided by government agencies and non-profit organizations dedicated to financial literacy education.

Uncovering Hidden Savings: Identifying and Trimming Unnecessary Expenses:

Identifying and reducing unnecessary expenses is a strategic approach to optimizing your budget, maximizing savings, and achieving your financial goals faster. By meticulously scrutinizing your spending habits and making conscious adjustments, you can free up resources for more meaningful pursuits.

Review Financial Services:

Evaluate fees associated with your bank accounts, credit cards, and other financial services. Consider switching to institutions that offer lower fees or better interest rates.

__Review Bank Statements:__

Regularly review your bank and credit card statements to identify any unauthorized or incorrect charges. Address discrepancies promptly.

Debt management and financial literacy go hand in hand in creating a solid foundation for your financial well-being. By effectively managing debt and continuously enhancing your financial knowledge, you gain the tools and confidence to make informed financial decisions, achieve your goals, and navigate the complexities of personal finance successfully. As you embark on your journey to financial literacy, remember that small steps toward education and proactive debt management can lead to significant improvements in your financial future. Identifying and reducing unnecessary expenses requires a deliberate shift in mindset and behavior. By cultivating financial mindfulness and consistently evaluating your spending habits, you empower yourself to make intentional choices that align with your goals. Remember that every dollar saved brings you closer to financial freedom, enabling you to allocate resources toward your priorities and dreams. As you trim unnecessary expenses, you embark on a journey of greater financial efficiency and resilience, ultimately shaping a future of increased wealth and well-being.

Chapter 7

Case Studies: Examples of Successful Strategies

Case studies provide different examples of wealth acceleration strategies in action. Here are a few illustrative scenarios showcasing how individuals used various approaches to accelerate their wealth:

❖ **Case Study 1: Real Estate Investment:**

Background:

Rabin, a software engineer, decided to invest in real estate as a means of wealth acceleration. He purchased a duplex property in an up-and-coming neighborhood.

Strategy:

Rabin lived in one unit and rented out the other. As the area developed, property values increased. After a few years, he sold the property for a significant profit.

Outcome:

Rabin's initial investment multiplied several times over, providing a substantial capital gain. He used the proceeds to reinvest in larger properties, ultimately building a diversified real estate portfolio and achieving financial independence.

❖ **Case Study 2: Entrepreneurial Success:**

Background:

Zuali, a skilled graphic designer, started a freelance design business from home.

Strategy:

She used social media and networking to attract clients and consistently delivered high-quality work. As her reputation grew, she expanded her business by hiring additional designers.

Outcome:

Zuali's business flourished, generating substantial revenue. She automated some processes and outsourced tasks, allowing her to focus on growth strategies. Her company became a thriving design agency, providing a steady stream of income and enabling her to achieve her wealth goals.

❖ Case Study 3: Investment Diversification:

Background:

Michael, a finance professional, was committed to building long-term wealth.

Strategy:

He diversified his investments across stocks, bonds, real estate, and a small business venture. He maintained a balanced portfolio, regularly rebalancing to manage risk.

Outcome:

Despite market fluctuations, Michael's diversified investments provided consistent returns over time. He was able to weather market downturns and capture opportunities for growth. His patient approach to investment yielded significant wealth accumulation.

❖ Case Study 4: Multiple Income Streams:

Background:

Emma, a marketing specialist, sought ways to increase her income.

Strategy:

In addition to her full-time job, Emma started a blog where she shared her marketing expertise. She monetized the blog through affiliate marketing and sponsored content. She also wrote an e-book and created online courses.

Outcome:

Emma's multiple income streams, including her job, blog, and digital products, steadily increased her earnings. She used the additional income to pay off debt, invest, and achieve her financial goals more quickly.

❖ **Case Study 5: Retirement Planning:**

Background:

David, a middle-aged professional, was concerned about his retirement.

Strategy:

He engaged a financial advisor who helped him create a comprehensive retirement plan. David maximized contributions to retirement accounts and invested in a diversified mix of assets.

Outcome:

Through disciplined saving and investing, David's retirement portfolio grew substantially. He was able to retire comfortably at his desired age, with a reliable stream of income to support his lifestyle.

These case studies demonstrate that wealth acceleration is achievable through a combination of strategic planning, dedication, and a willingness to explore diverse opportunities. While the specific strategies may vary, the underlying principles of smart investing, entrepreneurship, diversification, and proactive financial planning remain consistent. By tailoring these strategies to your unique circumstances and goals, you can embark on a path toward accelerated wealth accumulation and financial freedom.

Chapter 8

<u>Inspiring Real-Life Success Stories</u>

In this chapter, we will explore a variety of real-life success stories from individuals around the world who have achieved remarkable success in wealth management and acceleration. By examining their journeys, strategies, and lessons learned, you can gain valuable insights and inspiration for your own path toward financial prosperity. Let us delve into these compelling examples that showcase diverse approaches to wealth management and acceleration. These inspiring individuals started with minimal resources and overcame challenges to achieve remarkable financial success. Their stories highlight the power of determination, innovation, and strategic planning.

1. Warren Buffett - The Oracle of Omaha

Warren Buffett, one of the world's most renowned investors, built his wealth through disciplined value investing. He started with a small sum of money and patiently invested in undervalued companies, allowing compound interest to work its magic over decades. Buffett's story emphasizes the importance of patience, long-term thinking, and the power of compounding. He is super rich because he picks good companies to invest in and holds onto them for a long time. He also gives really good advice about money and investing. People really look up to him for his smart moves with money. Warren Buffett's famous quote is :

"If you don't find a way to make money while you sleep, you'll work until you die"

The quote emphasizes the importance of passive income and investments in achieving financial security and independence. It suggests that if you solely rely on active income (working during waking hours), you may have to continue working indefinitely. On the other hand, finding ways to generate income while you are not actively working, such as through investments or business ventures, can lead to greater financial freedom and the ability to build wealth over time.

Warren Buffett has a few simple principles for making money:

1. **Invest in What You Understand:** He suggests investing in companies and industries you know about. If you do not understand something, it's better to avoid investing in it.
2. **Long-Term Thinking:** Buffett believes in holding onto investments for a long time, sometimes even decades. He is not into quick buying and selling.
3. **Buy Quality Companies:** He looks for companies with strong and reliable earnings, good management, and competitive advantage.
4. **Margin of Safety:** Buffett likes to buy stocks when they're selling for less than what he thinks they're actually worth. This gives a "margin of safety" in case things do not go as planned.
5. **Avoid Timing the Market**: He advises against trying to predict when the stock market will go up or down. Instead, focus on the quality of the investments.
6. **Be Patient:** Buffett says patience is key. He does not rush into investments and waits for the right opportunities.
7. **Limit Debt:** He's not a fan of borrowing money to invest. He prefers to use his own money.

Continuous Learning: Buffett is always learning about new things. He reads a lot to stay updated on businesses and the economy.

Strategy:

Warren Buffett began investing at a young age, focusing on value investing principles. He consistently sought undervalued companies with strong fundamentals. Over time, his disciplined approach and patience led him to become one of the world's wealthiest individuals.

Statement:

"The stock market is a device for transferring money from the impatient to the patient."

2. Oprah Winfrey - From Rags to Riches

Oprah Winfrey's journey from a challenging upbringing to becoming a media mogul, philanthropist, and billionaire illustrates the significance of determination and resilience. By leveraging her unique skills, she built a media empire and diversified her income through various ventures, including television, magazines, and endorsements. Oprah's steadfast belief in her ability to overcome adversity and make a meaningful impact guided her journey. Her conviction that her past did not dictate her future became a driving force that propelled her to break barriers and inspire millions.

Strategy:

Oprah Winfrey began her career as a radio host and news anchor. Her breakthrough came when she hosted a local talk show that gained popularity. She leveraged her platform to establish her own production company and launched *"The Oprah Winfrey Show,"* which became a massive success.

Statement:

3. Elon Musk - Innovating for Wealth Acceleration

Elon Musk's ventures, including Tesla and SpaceX, X Corp showcase the impact of innovation on wealth acceleration. Through disruptive technologies and bold visions, Musk transformed industries and generated substantial returns. His story emphasizes the potential rewards of pushing boundaries and pursuing ground-breaking ideas.

Strategy:

Elon Musk co-founded Neuralink and OpenAI providing him with initial capital. He then ventured into electric cars with Tesla and space exploration with SpaceX. Musk's innovative approach and willingness to take on audacious challenges have been key to his success.

Statement:

"When something is important enough, you do it even if the odds are not in your favor."

4. Aliko Dangote-Building an African Empire

Aliko Dangote, the richest person in Africa, built his wealth through strategic investments in industries like cement, sugar, and flour. His story demonstrates the value of identifying local opportunities and leveraging them for substantial financial growth.

Strategy:

Aliko Dangote's strategy revolves around investing in key industries to foster economic growth and development in Africa. His approach includes:

1. **Industry Diversification:** Dangote has diversified his investments across sectors such as cement, sugar, salt, flour, and agriculture. This diversification minimizes risk and contributes to the growth of various sectors simultaneously.

2. **Local Production:** He focuses on promoting local production over imports. By establishing industries that manufacture essential goods within Africa, he aims to reduce the continent's reliance on foreign imports.

3. **Infrastructure Development:** Dangote's investments often involve building and upgrading infrastructure. This includes constructing cement plants, refineries, and distribution networks, which not only create jobs but also contribute to the development of necessary infrastructure.

4. **Job Creation:** A core aspect of his strategy is creating employment opportunities. By investing in labor-intensive industries, Dangote generates jobs, helping to alleviate unemployment and poverty in the regions where his businesses operate.

5. **African Expansion:** Dangote's vision extends beyond Nigeria. He seeks to replicate his success in other African countries, contributing to the economic growth and development of the entire continent.

Statement:

"Diversification and industrialization are the keys to unlocking Africa's potential. We must invest in sectors that will not only create jobs but also reduce our reliance on imports. By building industries and producing locally, we can achieve sustainable growth and transform the continent."

5. Sara Blakely-Creating a Global Brand

Sara Blakely, the founder of Spanx, revolutionized the shapewear industry and became a self-made billionaire. Her story highlights the significance of identifying gaps in the market, taking calculated risks, and maintaining a relentless focus on innovation.

Strategy:

Sara Blakely started Spanx with $5,000 and a revolutionary idea for shapewear. She faced multiple rejections from manufacturers before finding one to produce her product. Blakely's perseverance and focus on creating a solution led to Spanx becoming a billion-dollar business.

Statement:

"I think failure is nothing more than life's way of nudging you that you are off course. My attitude to failure is not attached to the outcome, but to not trying. It is liberating."

6. Li Ka-Shing - Diversified Business Ventures

Li Ka-Shing, a Hong Kong business magnate, diversified his investments across various sectors, including real estate, retail, and telecommunications. His story emphasizes the benefits of diversification and seizing opportunities in different industries.

Strategy:

In terms of diversified business ventures, Li Ka-shing is known for his strategy of investing in a wide range of industries. He established a conglomerate called Hutchison Whampoa, which later became CK Hutchison Holdings, that spans sectors like telecommunications, real estate, retail, energy, and more. This diversification helped him spread risk and capitalize on various market opportunities.

Statement:

"Vision is perhaps our greatest strength... it has kept us alive to the power and continuity of thought through the

centuries, it makes us peer into the future and lends shape to the unknown."

7. Robert Kiyosaki - The Power of Financial Education

Author and entrepreneur Robert Kiyosaki transformed his financial life by acquiring financial education and applying sound principles. His story underscores the importance of continuous learning, making informed decisions, and adopting a growth-oriented mindset.

Strategy:

Robert Kiyosaki's strategy revolves around the concept of financial education. He emphasizes that acquiring financial knowledge and understanding how money works is crucial for achieving financial success. Kiyosaki's *"Rich Dad, Poor Dad"* series emphasizes the importance of investing, entrepreneurship, and making informed financial decisions to achieve financial independence and wealth. He believes that learning about assets, liabilities, and passive income can empower individuals to make better financial choices.

Statement:

"The single most powerful asset we all have is our mind. If it is trained well, it can create enormous wealth in what seems to be an instant."

8. Sheryl Sandberg - Navigating Corporate Success

Sheryl Sandberg exemplifies the impact of climbing the corporate ladder and advocating for women's empowerment in the workplace. Her story showcases the significance of mentorship, leadership, and seizing career opportunities.

Statement:

"What would you do if you weren't afraid?"

Strategy:

Sheryl Sandberg is known for her strategy of advocating for women's empowerment and leadership in the workplace. She encourages women to lean in, take on challenges, and pursue their career goals with confidence. Sandberg's book *"Lean In"* emphasizes the importance of self-belief, negotiation skills, and breaking down gender barriers to achieve success in both professional and personal life. She also stresses the value of mentorship, networking, and supporting one another to create more inclusive and diverse work environments.

9. Richard Branson - Entrepreneurial Ventures

Richard Branson's journey from founding Virgin Records to expanding into multiple industries demonstrates the potential of entrepreneurial endeavors. His story highlights the value of creativity, adaptability, and daring to pursue unconventional ideas.

Strategy:

Richard Branson started his entrepreneurial journey with a mail-order record business. He diversified into music stores, airlines, telecommunications, and more. Branson's adventurous spirit and willingness to take calculated risks led to the growth of the Virgin Group.

Statement:

"I think it's quite great to set yourself a big challenge, and then you've got another reason for keeping fit."

10. Ratan Tata - Legacy of Business Leadership

Ratan Tata, former chairman of Tata Group, navigated complex business challenges and expanded the conglomerate's global presence. His story showcases the importance of ethical leadership, strategic decision-making, and a commitment to long-term success.

Strategy:

Ratan Tata is known for his strategic leadership and transformative vision for the Tata Group. His strategy involves innovation, global expansion, and social responsibility. Under his leadership, Tata Group diversified into various industries such as automobiles, information technology, steel, and more. Tata's commitment to ethical business practices and community development is reflected in initiatives like the Tata Nano car project and the Tata Trusts, which focus on philanthropic efforts. His emphasis on long-term thinking and adapting to changing times has been a cornerstone of his approach to business.

Statement:

"I don't believe in taking the right decisions. I take decisions and then make them right."

11. Gisele Bündchen - Diversified Income Streams

Supermodel Gisele Bündchen diversified her income through modeling, endorsements, and eco-friendly business ventures. Her story emphasizes the potential of building multiple income streams and using fame as a platform for positive impact.

Strategy:

Her strategy seems to be centered around professionalism, hard work, and maintaining a healthy lifestyle. Throughout her career, she has been a prominent advocate for sustainability and environmental causes, using her platform to promote eco-friendly practices and conscious consumerism.

Statement:

"The quality of life depends on the quality of your thoughts."

12. Success Story: Chris Gardner - From Homelessness to Wealth

Chris Gardner's journey from homelessness to a successful stockbroker, as depicted in the movie *"The Pursuit of Happyness,"* underscores the significance of determination, resilience, and unwavering belief in one is potential.

Strategy:

Chris Gardner is known for his strategy of persistence, determination, and resilience. His strategy involves facing challenges head-on, maintaining a positive attitude, and never giving up on his goals. Gardner's emphasis on hard work, adaptability, and the pursuit of one's passion has inspired many to overcome adversity and pursue their dreams.

Statement:

"The secret to success: finds something you love to do so much; you can't wait for the sun to rise to do it all over again."

These success stories illustrate diverse paths to wealth management and acceleration. From investment strategies to entrepreneurship, each example offers valuable lessons and insights that you can apply to your own financial journey. By studying the experiences of these individuals, you can gain inspiration, guidance, and a deeper understanding of the principles that contribute to financial success. Remember, while each journey is unique, the underlying principles of determination, smart decision-making, and continuous learning are universal keys to achieving your wealth-building goals.

These individuals exemplify the transformative power of determination, innovation, and resilience. Their journeys from humble beginnings to financial success underscore the importance of embracing challenges, learning from failures, and pursuing a vision with unwavering commitment. By taking calculated risks, thinking creatively, and persevering through adversity, these *"heroes"* of financial success have left a lasting legacy that continues to inspire others to chase their dreams.

Conclusion: A Journey of Transformation

Embracing the journey to financial freedom has been a transformative experience, one that has enriched not only my bank account but also my mindset and outlook on life. The commitment to lifelong learning and continuous improvement has been my compass, guiding me through challenges, setbacks, and triumphs. With each step forward, I am reminded that the pursuit of financial freedom is not merely a destination, but a journey of self-discovery, empowerment, and lasting impact.

Acting Today for a Prosperous Tomorrow

The key to achieving a prosperous tomorrow lies in the actions we take today. By making deliberate and strategic choices now, we pave the way for a future filled with financial stability, growth, and abundance. Here is how acting today can shape a prosperous tomorrow:

1. Setting Clear Goals:

Define your short-term and long-term financial goals. Establish specific, measurable, achievable, relevant, and time-bound (SMART) objectives. These goals provide direction and purpose, motivating you to stay on track.

2. Building a Solid Foundation:

Focus on building a strong financial foundation. Start by creating an emergency fund to cover unexpected expenses. Pay off high-interest debt to reduce financial burdens and free up resources for saving and investing.

3. Budgeting and Financial Planning:

Create a realistic budget that aligns with your goals and priorities. Track your income, expenses, and savings diligently. A well-structured budget enables you to manage your money effectively and make informed financial decisions.

4. Investing Early and Consistently:

Begin investing early to harness the power of compounding. Regular contributions to retirement accounts, stocks, bonds, or other investment vehicles can lead to significant growth over time. Consistency is key.

5. Embracing Financial Literacy:

Invest in your financial education. Continuously expand your knowledge about personal finance, investments, taxes, and wealth-building strategies. Informed decisions are more likely to yield favorable outcomes.

6. Managing Risks:

Mitigate risks by obtaining appropriate insurance coverage, including health, life, and property insurance. Being prepared for unforeseen events safeguards your financial stability and minimizes potential setbacks.

7. Diversifying Income Streams:

Explore opportunities to generate multiple income streams. This could involve a side business, freelancing, or investments that generate passive income. Diversification enhances financial security and flexibility.

8. Controlling Spending Habits:

Practice mindful spending by distinguishing between needs and wants. Avoid impulse purchases and prioritize expenses that align with your goals. A conscious approach to spending contributes to saving and investing.

9. Continuously Evaluating Progress:

Regularly assess your financial progress. Review your goals, track your net worth, and analyze your investment performance. Adjust your strategies as needed to stay aligned with your evolving aspirations.

10. Staying Adaptable:

Flexibility is essential. Life circumstances change, and markets fluctuate. Stay adaptable and open to adjusting your plans when necessary. Being willing to pivot ensures that you remain on the path to prosperity.

11. Fostering a Positive Mindset:

Cultivate a positive attitude toward money and wealth. Visualize your goals, affirm your success, and embrace a mindset of abundance. A positive outlook enhances your motivation and resilience.

12. Taking Small Steps Consistently:

Remember that progress is achieved through consistent, incremental steps. Act daily, no matter how small, toward your financial goals. These small efforts compound over time and contribute to your prosperous future.

Building Your Future Today:

The decisions you make and the actions you take today have a profound impact on the prosperity you will experience tomorrow. By focusing on your goals, practicing financial discipline, and remaining committed to continuous growth, you create a solid foundation for a future filled with financial well-being, opportunities, and fulfillment. Start today, and watch as your efforts transform into a prosperous and abundant tomorrow.

By focusing on both building and protecting your wealth, you are creating a solid foundation for a secure and prosperous future. Through strategic investments, prudent financial decisions, and effective risk management, you can achieve your financial aspirations and leave a positive impact for generations to come. Remember, building and protecting wealth is a lifelong journey, and by implementing these simple

yet impactful strategies, you are taking meaningful steps toward
lasting financial security.

Would you kindly consider leaving a review for the book?

One last time!

Your feedback is immensely valuable, especially for authors like me who lack a significant following. Reviews play a vital role in expanding my readership by encouraging others to explore my books.

Reviews truly are the lifeblood of any author.

Sharing your thoughts would only take a brief moment, yet it would greatly assist me in reaching a wider audience.

I appreciate your support and would be delighted to read your review of the book. If you could send your review via email to **franksd17@hotmail.com**, it would mean a lot.

Thank you for your time and consideration.